SEVEN SUMMITS

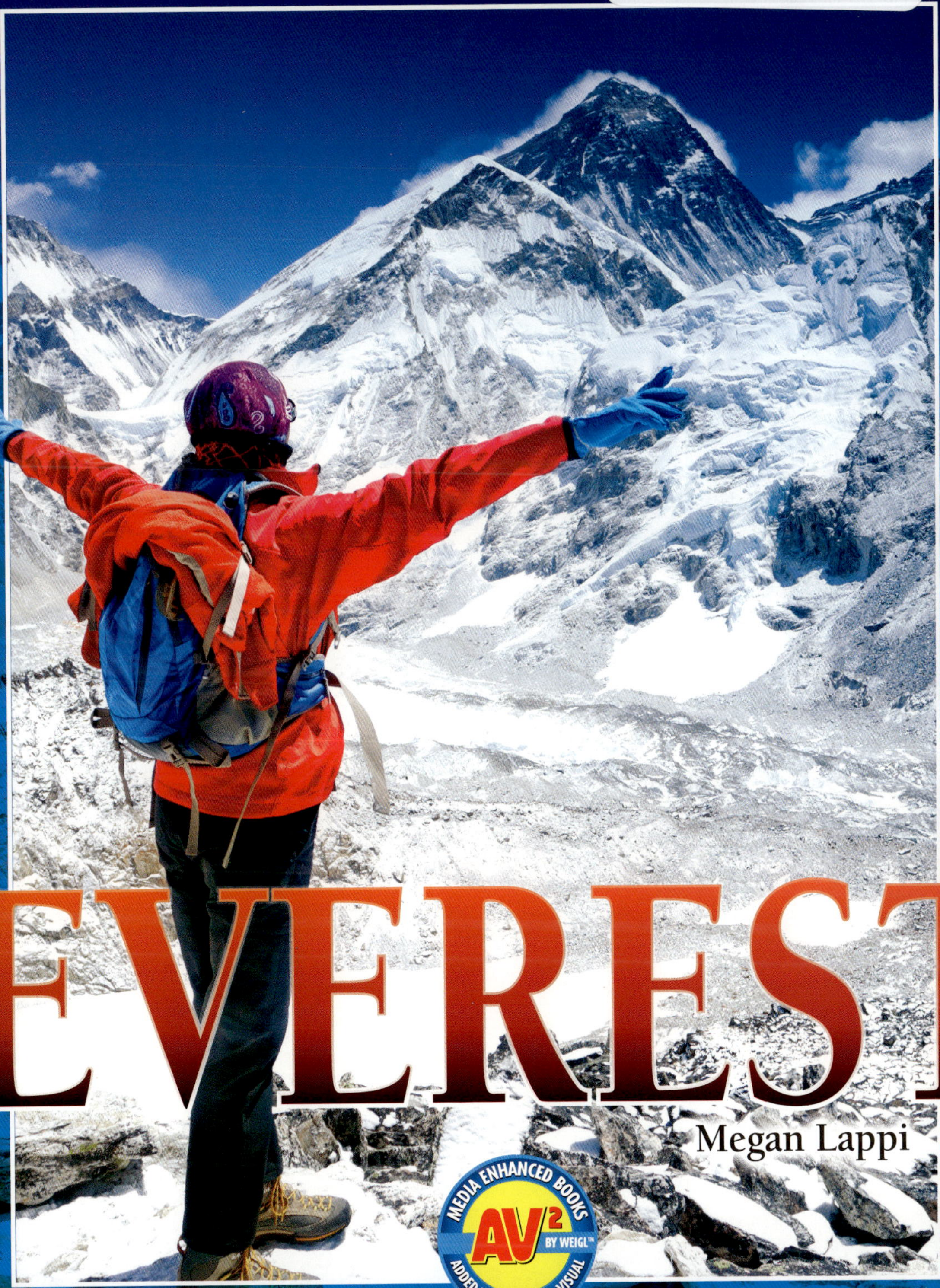

EVEREST

Megan Lappi

MEDIA ENHANCED BOOKS
AV2 BY WEIGL
ADDED VALUE • AUDIO VISUAL

www.av2books.com

Go to www.av2books.com, and enter this book's unique code.

BOOK CODE

AVY52757

AV² by Weigl brings you media enhanced books that support active learning.

AV² provides enriched content that supplements and complements this book. Weigl's AV² books strive to create inspired learning and engage young minds in a total learning experience.

Your AV² Media Enhanced books come alive with...

Audio
Listen to sections of the book read aloud.

Video
Watch informative video clips.

Embedded Weblinks
Gain additional information for research.

Try This!
Complete activities and hands-on experiments.

Key Words
Study vocabulary, and complete a matching word activity.

Quizzes
Test your knowledge.

Slideshow
View images and captions, and prepare a presentation.

... and much, much more!

Published by AV2 by Weigl
350 5th Avenue, 59th Floor
New York, NY 10118
Website: www.av2books.com

Library of Congress Cataloging-in-Publication Data
Names: Lappi, Megan, author.
Title: Everest / Megan Lappi.
Description: New York : AV2 by Weigl, [2019] | Series: Seven summits | Includes index. | Audience: Grade 4 to 6.
Identifiers: LCCN 2019009596 (print) | LCCN 2019016831 (ebook) | ISBN 9781791114251 (multi User ebook) | ISBN 9781791114268 (single User ebook) | ISBN 9781791114237 (hardcover : alk. paper) | ISBN 9781791114244 (softcover : alk. paper)
Subjects: LCSH: Everest, Mount (China and Nepal)--Juvenile literature.
Classification: LCC DS495.8.E9 (ebook) | LCC DS495.8.E9 L37 2019 (print) | DDC 954.96--dc23
LC record available at https://lccn.loc.gov/2019009596

Printed in Guangzhou, China
1 2 3 4 5 6 7 8 9 23 22 21 20 19

052019
102318

Project Coordinator Heather Kissock
Designers Tammy West and Ana Maria Vidal

Photo Credits
Weigl acknowledges Getty Images, Alamy, Shutterstock, and iStock as its primary photo suppliers for this title.

SEVEN SUMMITS

EVEREST

CONTENTS

The Highest Summit

To reach the top of Mount Everest is to stand on the top of the world. The summit, or top of the mountain, soars 29,035 feet (8,850 meters) in the air. Mount Everest, in the Himalaya Mountain Range, is the highest mountain in the world. People did not reach its peak until the mid-1900s.

Climbing Mount Everest tests the limits of human endurance. The unforgiving mountain threatens climbers with avalanches, high winds, and unbearably cold temperatures. People have difficulty breathing at the top of the mountain due to the thin air at that **altitude**. They suffer from the many symptoms of **altitude sickness**. Despite the pain they must endure, mountain climbers agree that reaching the world's highest mountaintop is an exciting experience.

Climbers sometimes need to use ladders to cross wide openings on the path to the summit of Mount Everest.

Tibetan prayer flags bring color to the harsh landscape. Tibetans believe that the positive images and writings on the flags are spread through the area by the wind.

MAP OF MOUNT EVEREST

MOUNT EVEREST FACTS

- Mount Everest is located in the country of Nepal. The Nepalese capital city, Kathmandu, is about 100 miles (161 kilometers) from the base of Mount Everest.
- The Nepalese people call Mount Everest *Sagarmatha*, which means "goddess of the sky."
- The Government of Nepal established Sagarmatha National Park in 1976. It is a protected area that includes Mount Everest.
- Despite cold temperatures and high altitude, people live around the base of Mount Everest. One of the largest ethnic groups is the Sherpa.
- The first people reached the top of Mount Everest in 1953, but the first person to climb to the top alone was Reinhold Messner, in 1980.
- Almost 300 people have died trying to climb Mount Everest. More than 200 bodies have been left behind on the mountain.

Where in the World?

Mount Everest is just one of the mountains in the Himalayas, a mountain range located mostly in Nepal. To the north of Everest lies the Tibet region of China. India is to the south.

The Himalaya Range is 1,550 miles (2,494 km) long.

Mount Everest is not the only huge mountain in the area. The Himalaya Range boasts 9 of the 10 highest mountains in the world. Just 100 miles (161 km) east of Everest stands Mount Kanchenjunga. At 28,169 feet (8,586 m), it is the third highest mountain in the world. To the west of the Himalayas, stretching into India, is the mighty Karakoram mountain range. The Karakoram boasts the world's second-highest mountain. It is called K2 and is 28,251 feet (8,611 m) high.

Even though K2 is shorter than Mount Everest, it is more difficult to climb because of bad weather.

Puzzler

Other regions of the world have major mountain ranges, but none of these ranges have mountains as high as Mount Everest.

Q: Can you locate these major mountain ranges on the map?

Alps
Andes Mountains
Caucasus Mountains
Rocky Mountains
Karakoram Mountains

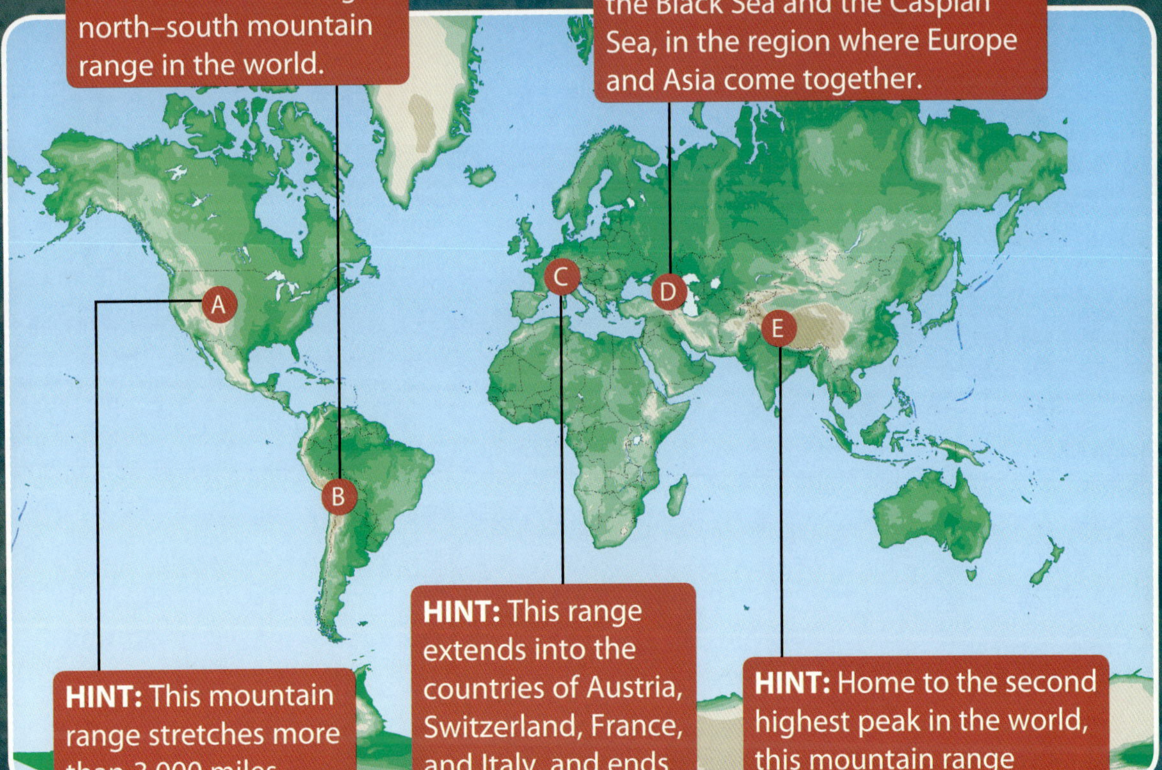

HINT: This is the longest north–south mountain range in the world.

HINT: This range lies between the Black Sea and the Caspian Sea, in the region where Europe and Asia come together.

HINT: This mountain range stretches more than 3,000 miles (4,800 km) from New Mexico to Alaska.

HINT: This range extends into the countries of Austria, Switzerland, France, and Italy, and ends in Albania, on the Adriatic Sea.

HINT: Home to the second highest peak in the world, this mountain range covers territory claimed by India, Pakistan, and China.

A: A. Rocky Mountains B. Andes Mountains C. Alps D. Caucasus Mountains E. Karakoram Mountains

A Trip Back in Time

Hundreds of millions of years ago, the Asian continent looked very different from its present shape. Its southern border was located where the Himalayas now stand. The land now called India was part of a huge landmass called Pangaea. About 200 million years ago, Pangaea separated into smaller pieces. These **tectonic plates** drifted in different directions. The Indian plate traveled north and eventually collided with the Eurasian plate, containing Asia and much of Europe. The Himalaya Mountains were formed as a result of the two landmasses colliding.

The Himalayas create a natural border between some of the countries on the Asian continent, including India, Nepal, Bhutan, and China.

When Plates Collide

The violent collision of tectonic plates can create mountain ranges, such as the Himalayas. Mountains do not develop immediately, though. They rise from the ground gradually, over millions of years.

When masses of land collide with each other, the two pieces do not instantly stop moving. As the plates grind against each other, their edges crumple like an accordion. Some of the massive rocks are forced up above the surface of the ground, becoming mountains. Although this grinding of plates has slowed significantly, the process continues today.

Geologists estimate that India continues to move north about 2 inches (5.08 centimeters) per year. This creates great stresses in the earth that sometimes result in earthquakes. Scientists work to predict when large earthquakes in the region might occur.

TECTONIC PLATES COLLISION

Millions of years ago, India split off from an ancient continent and began to move north. It collided with Eurasia.

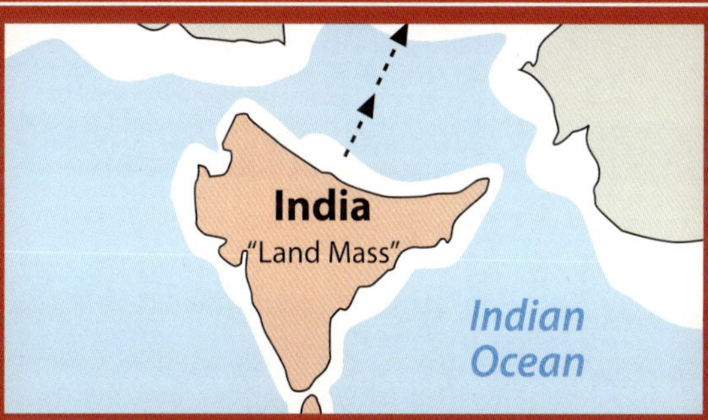

Within about 50 million years, the Himalaya Mountains arose due to the collision of the Indian and Eurasian Plates.

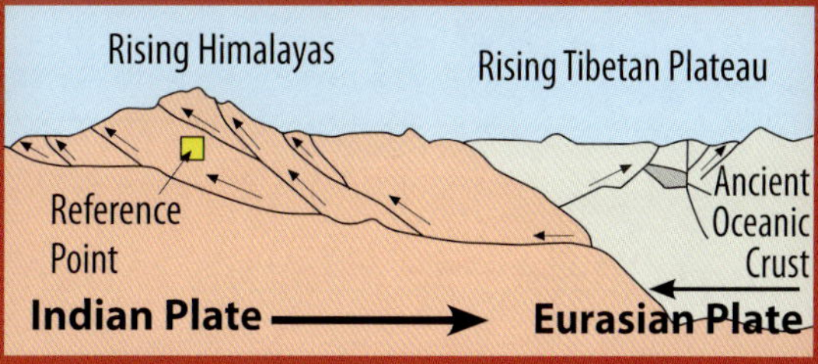

Today, the Indian and Eurasian Plates continue to collide.

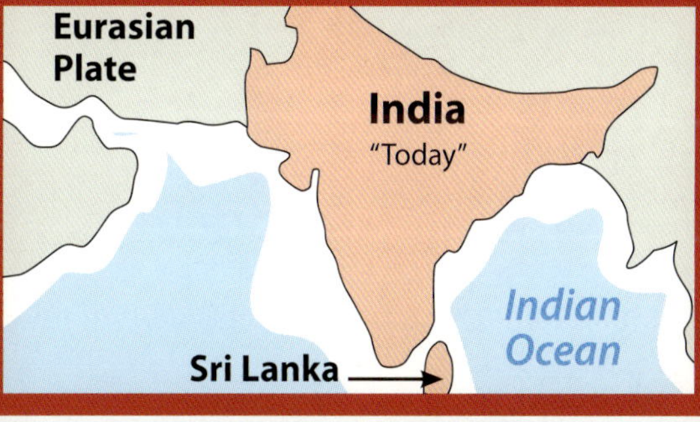

Weather on the Mountain

People do not visit Mount Everest for its weather. Mount Everest temperatures are very cold throughout the year. In the coldest winter month, January, the average temperature is an unbearable –33° Fahrenheit (–36° Celsius). Temperatures can even become as cold as –70°F (–57°C). The milder months bring little relief. The temperature never rises above the freezing point, 32°F (0°C), on the summit.

June through September is **monsoon** season, when tremendous storms arise from the Indian Ocean. Strong winds mix with heavy snow to create blizzards on Everest. Sudden storms and blasts of wind create hazards for mountain climbers.

The weather on Mount Everest is hard to predict. It can change from sunny to snowy within a few minutes.

How High Is Mount Everest?

The Mount Everest summit rises so high that it is the only place on Earth where a person can be exposed to winds from the jet stream. The jet stream is a system of fast-moving air currents in the upper part of the **troposphere**, a layer of Earth's **atmosphere**. Clouds, storms, and most weather take place in the troposphere. When jet streams hit Everest, climbers can be hit with wind gusts of 170 miles (274 km) per hour. Winds that strong can easily blow a person off the mountain.

The Earth's atmosphere has five layers. The troposphere is the thinnest layer. Even so, the planet's highest mountain does not reach the top of it.

LAYERS OF THE ATMOSPHERE

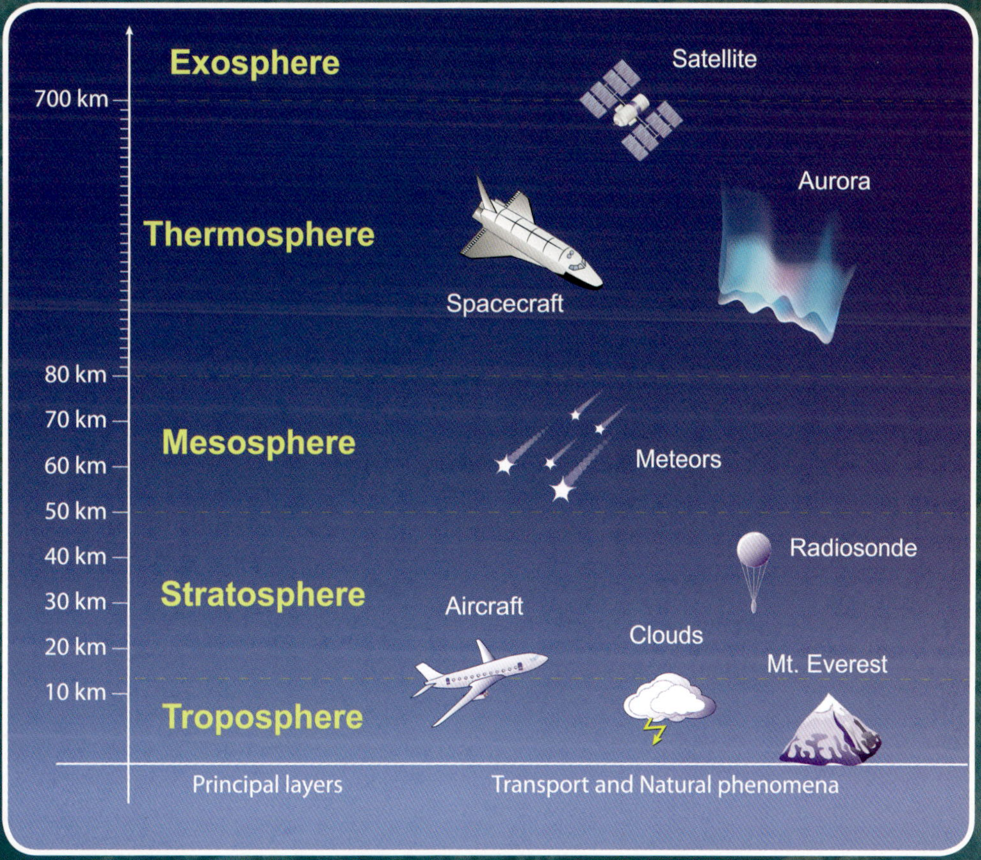

Life on the Mountain

Very few living things are able to survive on Mount Everest. Most of the mountain's plant life thrives below the **tree line**, at 11,000 feet (3,353 m). There, green forests are highlighted by bright colors from flowering plants, such as rhododendrons. Trees do not grow above the tree line due to the extreme cold and wind and the lack of soil, but grass and small bushes take root in rocky **crevices**. At higher elevations, only simple plants, such as moss and lichen, can grow on Everest's rocky surface.

The rhododendron is the national flower of Nepal.

The Everest snow line is located at 18,000 feet (5,486 m). Above this point, the mountain's surface is covered with ice and snow almost year-round. Plant and animal life are rarely found this high. Other than some tiny spiders discovered at 22,000 feet (6,706 m), the Everest summit is a desolate, lifeless place.

Only about 3 percent of Sagarmatha National Park is forested.

Useful Yaks

Below the tree line, many different types of animals live in the Everest area, from monkeys to bears to birds. Above the tree line, however, the altitude, cold, and lack of food from plants make survival difficult for many creatures. The yak is one of the few mammals that lives in this harsh mountain environment. These ox-like animals roam freely. They are also raised by farmers who live near the mountain.

Yaks are important to the humans who live on and visit Everest. With no roads allowing cars or trucks up the mountain, equipment and supplies must be carried up rough paths. Yaks can carry loads weighing more than 300 pounds (136 kilograms). Their strong hooves allow them to walk steadily on rock. Scientists have found that yaks have special lungs that allow these animals to thrive more easily at high altitudes than other animals.

Yaks are meant to live in high, cold locations. It is difficult for them to live comfortably in lower areas because of their thick coats.

Early Explorers

People have lived near Mount Everest for centuries, but historians are certain that they could not climb to its summit without 20th-century technology. In the mid-1800s, British **surveyors** noticed Mount Everest. A surveyor named George Everest was the first European to identify the exact location of the mountain. In 1865, it was named after him.

In the early 1900s, European adventurers began making serious attempts to climb Mount Everest. In 1924, British climbers George Mallory and Andrew Irvine climbed higher than anyone had in the past. Their mission ended in tragedy. They both died before they reached the summit. Mallory's frozen body was found on the mountain 75 years later.

The lure of reaching the world's highest peak inspired many other climbing attempts over the years. In 1953, two men finally reached the top. Edmund Hillary and Tenzing Norgay were the first humans to stand on Earth's highest point.

George Mallory also attempted to climb Mount Everest in 1922. His partner for that climb was Edward Norton.

Biography

Sir Edmund Hillary and Tenzing Norgay

In early 1953, New Zealander Edmund Hillary, a former beekeeper and navy navigator, joined a British-led expedition to Mount Everest. He was paired with Tenzing Norgay, a local guide who had more experience exploring Everest than any other team member.

The expedition took 6 weeks to climb from the base of the mountain to 27,900 feet (8,504 m), where they made camp. While their companions stayed at camp, Hillary and Norgay made the dangerous climb to the summit on May 29, 1953. Standing together atop the mountain, they took pictures and held a brief, 15-minute celebration.

Hillary and Norgay were recognized as heroes once the news of their feat reached the world. Norgay became one of the most famous people in Nepal. He spent the rest of his life teaching mountain climbing and working to improve living conditions for the Sherpa people. Queen Elizabeth II of England made Edmund Hillary a knight, adding the title of "Sir" to his name. He led many other expeditions in the Himalayas, as well as to the South Pole.

Edmund Hillary and Tenzing Norgay were 33 and 39 years old when they reached the summit of Mount Everest.

The Big Picture

The highest peaks on each of Earth's continents are called the "seven summits." Some climbers make it their goal to reach all seven peaks. This can take years of planning, training, and preparing.

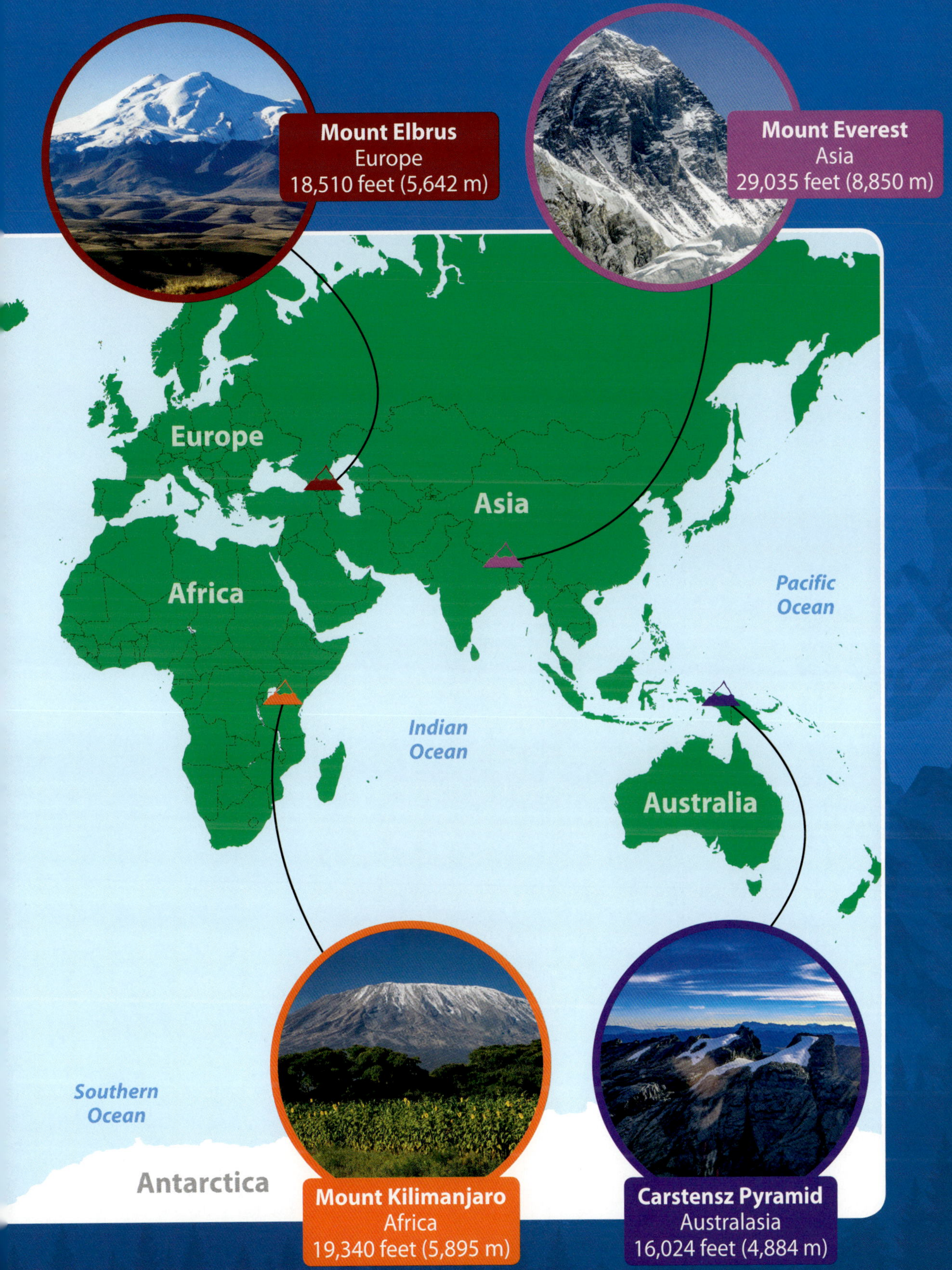
Mount Elbrus
Europe
18,510 feet (5,642 m)
Mount Everest
Asia
29,035 feet (8,850 m)
Europe
Asia
Africa
Pacific Ocean
Indian Ocean
Australia
Southern Ocean
Antarctica
Mount Kilimanjaro
Africa
19,340 feet (5,895 m)
Carstensz Pyramid
Australasia
16,024 feet (4,884 m)

People of the Mountain

Mount Everest is not an easy place to live, but people do make their homes in the lower altitudes of the Himalayas. Among the several ethnic groups who live in the region, the Sherpas are perhaps the best-known people of the mountains.

Sherpas traveled south to Nepal from Tibet approximately 600 years ago. About 70,000 Sherpas live in northeastern Nepal. They live in small villages, farm the land, and herd animals, such as goats and yaks. In recent decades, as more visitors traveled to Mount Everest, Sherpas have made their living as guides and porters. While the tourism industry has brought relative prosperity to the Sherpas, it has also brought problems. About 60 Sherpas who worked as porters or as guides have died on the mountain.

Potato is the crop most commonly grown by Sherpa farmers.

Helping Hands

Porters are crucial members of any expedition on Mount Everest. Every mountain-climbing team employs local porters to carry supplies. Porters live near Everest, so they know the landscape, the animals, and the weather better than anyone. Many porters are Sherpas, but the work is also performed by people from other ethnic groups, including the Rais and Limbu peoples.

Living their entire lives in high altitudes, porters have adapted to the thin mountain air. They are able to endure the weather and altitude. Porters have mastered the ability to carry huge supply packs up and down steep, dangerous mountain paths.

The average male porter carries packs that weigh almost as much as he does. Some can carry packs that weigh almost twice as much as their body weight.

Timeline

Prehistoric

40–50 million years ago Himalaya Mountains begin to form as tectonic plates collide.

2.6 million–11,000 years ago The Great Himalayas part of this mountain range begin to take their present-day shape.

Exploration

1852 British surveyors determine that Everest is the world's highest mountain.

1865 Mount Everest is named after Sir George Everest, the first surveyor to map the mountain.

1922 Everest climbers first use oxygen tanks.

1924 George Mallory and Andrew Irvine die during their attempted Everest climb.

1951 Edmund Hillary joins his first expedition to Mount Everest.

1952 Tenzing Norgay is part of an Everest climb that reaches 28,210 feet (8,598 m), the highest altitude reached to date.

1953 Edmund Hillary and Tenzing Norgay become the first climbers to reach Everest's summit.

1975 Japan's Junko Tabei is the first woman to reach the summit.

Development

1976 Sagarmatha National Park is established to protect Everest's environment.

1978 Reinhold Messner and Peter Habeler are the first people to reach the summit without oxygen tanks.

1996 Fifteen people die trying to climb Mount Everest, a one-year record number of deaths on the mountain.

1999 George Mallory's frozen body is found on Everest, 75 years after his death.

Present

2004 A 45-year-old climber named Apa Sherpa completes his 14th Everest climb, the most climbs by any person in history.

2005 French test pilot Didier Delsalle lands a helicopter on the summit of Everest.

2007 British hiker Rod Baber makes the first phone call and sends the first text message from the summit of Everest.

2010 A 13-year-old boy from the United States, Jordan Romero, becomes the youngest person ever to reach the summit of Everest.

2018 Xia Boyu, a 69-year-old from China, becomes the first double amputee to reach the summit of Everest from the Nepal side.

Key Issue: Cleaning Up Everest

Prior to the 20th century, there were very few visitors to Mount Everest. In the past decade, however, the tourist industry has grown dramatically. In 2018, Nepal had a record number of more than 1 million tourists. Mount Everest also had 807 climbers reach the summit in 2018, the highest number ever. The people who come to climb Everest risk their own lives, as well as those of their traveling companions. They also threaten the local environment by leaving trash behind. Even though the Nepalese government has imposed strict rules requiring visitors to keep the peak clean, tons of garbage have accumulated on the mountain. Recent estimates indicate that there may be about 150 tons (136 tonnes) of trash on Mount Everest.

Each Everest expedition lasts several weeks, so every climber creates garbage. Snow has covered empty oxygen bottles, old ropes, food and food packaging, and old tents. Climbers leave behind papers, plastics, and metals. Even the frozen, dead bodies of climbers remain on Mount Everest. Few objects **decompose** in the extreme cold and high altitudes of Mount Everest.

Melting ice is now exposing decades' worth of trash that was previously hidden.

Efforts have begun to clean up the mountain, which has sometimes been called the world's highest garbage pit. In 2014, Nepal's tourism ministry requested that all climbers bring an additional 18 pounds (8.2 kg) of garbage back at the end of their climb. In 2018, a national cleanup campaign set a goal of removing 100 tons (91 tonnes) of trash from the mountain that year. Still, trash remains. Volunteers will continue their efforts, and climbers will be asked to take their trash with them. The goal is to make Mount Everest as pristine as it was when the first climbers began their ascent.

Climbers on the Tibet side of Everest are also asked to bring 18 pounds (8.2 kg) of garbage back with them. They are fined $100 per every 2.2 pounds (1 kg) that they do not bring back.

SHOULD CLIMBERS BE ALLOWED TO CLIMB MOUNT EVEREST?

YES	NO
Most climbers are responsible and remove their own garbage.	Some irresponsible climbers leave garbage behind.
Assisting climbers provides a living for Sherpas and other local people.	Even with Sherpa guides, some inexperienced climbers risk their lives by climbing the dangerous mountain.
People should be allowed to experience one of the world's greatest wonders.	Mount Everest can be enjoyed from a safe distance.

The Dangers of Visiting Everest

Perhaps the greatest danger facing Everest climbers is the air. The low **air pressure** of high altitudes does not allow people to receive enough oxygen when they breathe. With too little oxygen, people can suffer from altitude sickness. This condition can cause problems such as headaches, dizziness, vomiting, and **hallucinations**. The brain does not function properly without oxygen, so people find it difficult to complete simple tasks, such as tying shoelaces. More complex mountain-climbing tasks can result in fatal accidents.

An Everest climb must be taken slowly. At 17,600 feet (5,364 m) is the base camp, where climbers stop and rest for a day or two. As they continue climbing, people stop to rest for a day or more at intervals of 2,000 to 3,000 feet (610 to 914 m). This process of regular rest stops allows the body to adjust to a new altitude before moving upward. The entire journey up and down the mountain lasts about 3 weeks. To attempt climbing any faster could be deadly.

The changes in weather also make Mount Everest dangerous for climbers. Avalanches can happen after a snowstorm. People can be buried under feet of snow, or blown off their feet by strong gusts of wind.

Death Zone

The final 3,000 feet (914 m) leading to Everest's summit is called the "death zone," because this is the most dangerous place for humans climbing the mountain. At this elevation, climbers cannot avoid altitude sickness. They simply must deal with its symptoms. To help overcome the lack of oxygen, climbers carry oxygen tanks and breathe through masks. A few daredevil climbers have actually climbed to the summit without oxygen tanks, but this is a highly dangerous feat.

Once climbers reach the summit, they do not usually stay there very long. After a few photographs and handshakes, it is time to start climbing down. People need to complete their stay in the death zone in 2 or 3 days. Spending any more time at this extreme altitude could prove fatal to even the most experienced mountain climbers.

Eye protection is an important part of climbing gear. In the death zone, snow blindness can cause people to temporarily lose their vision.

Stories from the Mountain

For more than a century, brave and adventuresome men and women have climbed Mount Everest. Many stories of triumph have emerged from these treks, but there are also stories of tragedy. The summit has been reached more than 8,000 times, but nearly 300 people have died trying.

In 1996, journalist Jon Krakauer attempted to climb Everest with a group of climbers from all over the world. Eight members of the group died in a sudden snowstorm. At the time, it was Everest's greatest recorded disaster. Krakauer told the story in a best-selling book called *Into Thin Air*.

More disaster struck in 2014 and 2015. An avalanche in April 2014 took the lives of 16 Nepalese guides. In April 2015, a nearby earthquake caused an avalanche at the Everest Base Camp that killed at least 22 people. This became the deadliest year on Mount Everest.

The avalanche that hit the Everest Base Camp in 2015 destroyed most of the camp's medical equipment.

Legend of the Yeti

There have been many stories told over the years about the Yeti, also called the Abominable Snowman. According to legend, the Yeti is a half-man, half-ape creature that lives in the Himalayas. In 1951, explorer Eric Shipton took photos of giant footprints in the snow. He claimed these were the tracks of the Yeti, but his claim was never proven true or false.

Over the past 50 years, other people have reported seeing a creature similar to the Yeti on Mount Everest. The Yeti's legend continues to grow, but no hard evidence has been discovered to prove the Yeti exists. Non-believers think that most Yeti sightings are actually bears.

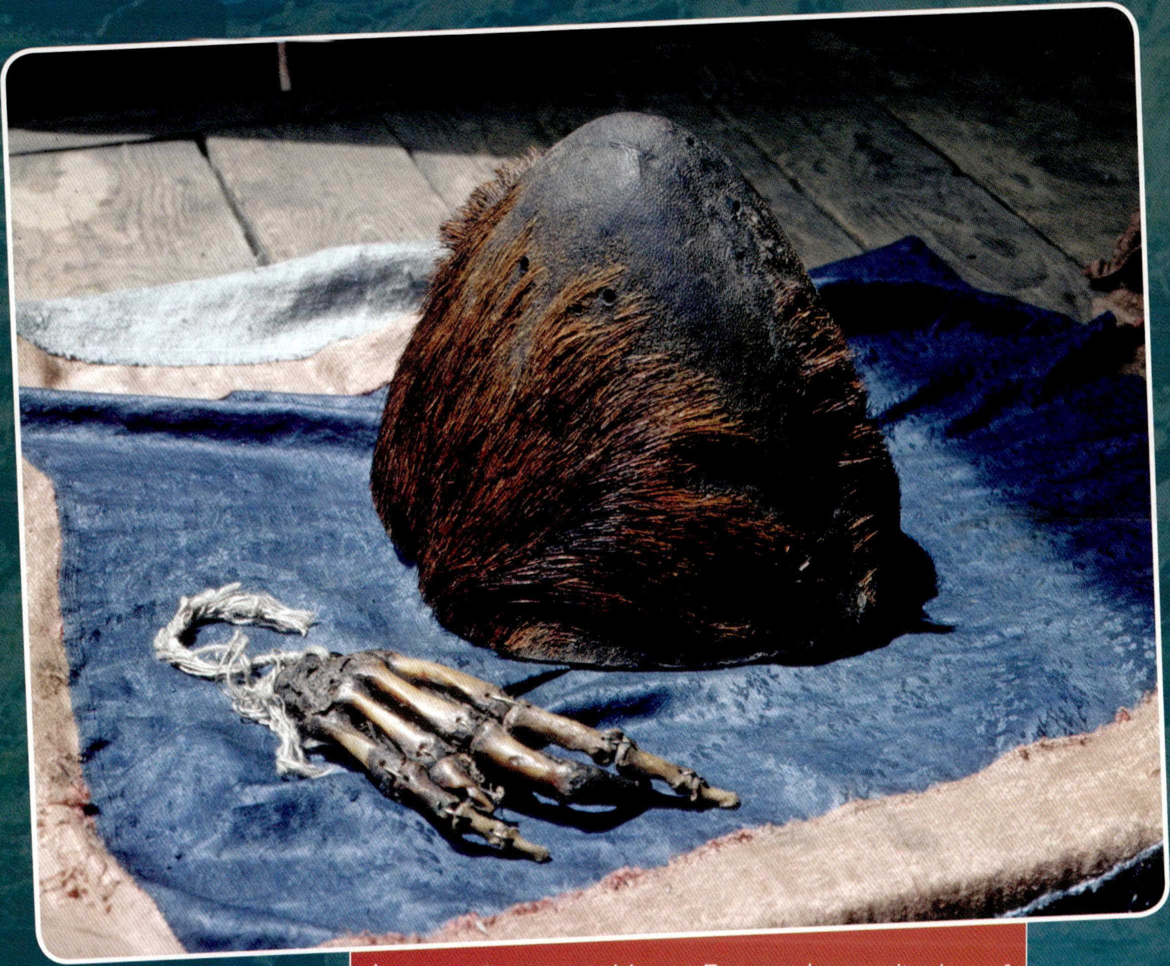

A monastery near Mount Everest has a display of what some people claim is a Yeti skull and hand.

What Have You Learned?

True or False?

Decide whether the following statements are true or false. If the statement is false, make it true.

1

Mount Everest is named after the person who first climbed to its peak.

2

K2 is a mountain located in the Himalayas.

3

Temperatures on Everest can drop as low as -70°F (-57°C).

4

Scientists have proof that the Yeti exists.

5

Sir Edmund Hillary reached the Everest summit by himself.

6

People need to complete their stay in the death zone in 2 or 3 days.

ANSWERS

1. False. The mountain is named for Sir George Everest. He first surveyed the mountain.
2. False. K2 is located in the Karakoram mountain range. **3.** True
4. False. There is no proof that the Yeti, or Abominable Snowman, exists.
5. False. Hillary and Tenzing Norgay reached the summit together. **6.** True

Short Answer

Answer the following questions using information from the book.

1. **Who wrote the book *Into Thin Air*?**
2. **Which animals are used for carrying heavy loads of supplies on Mount Everest?**
3. **What is the highest mountain in Africa?**
4. **What country is home to Mount Everest?**
5. **Who died trying to climb Mount Everest in 1924?**

ANSWERS
1. Jon Krakauer **2.** Yaks **3.** Mount Kilimanjaro **4.** Nepal **5.** George Mallory and Andrew Irvine

Multiple Choice

Choose the best answer for the following questions.

1. **Tenzing Norgay was a member of which ethnic group?**
   a. Limbu
   b. Rais
   c. Sherpa

2. **What is Sir Edmund Hillary's native country?**
   a. England
   b. United States
   c. New Zealand

3. **What is the summit of a mountain?**
   a. The very bottom
   b. The very top
   c. The snow line

4. **What has been the deadliest year for climbers on Mount Everest?**
   a. 1996
   b. 2015
   c. 1953

ANSWERS
1. c **2.** c **3.** b **4.** b

Activity

When Plates Collide

When two equally dense masses of land collide, rock is usually forced upward. This is called a convergent boundary. Today, as India moves northward, the collision with the Asian plate continues. Try this experiment to see how convergent boundaries are created.

Materials

1 hard-boiled egg

water-based marker

Instructions

1. Tap the egg gently until it has several cracks.
2. Trace along the major cracks with the marker.
3. Gently squeeze the egg until the shell pieces start to move.
4. Look for places where two pieces of eggshell are colliding.

Results

The pieces will be pushed up. This represents a convergent boundary. On Earth, one tectonic plate will fold and deform, turning into a mountain range. This is what happened millions of years ago when the Himalayas were formed. Two plates collided with each other, forcing rock up and creating the mountain range.

Key Words

air pressure: the pressure, or force, created by the weight of the air

altitude: the measurement above sea level of different locations on Earth

altitude sickness: headaches, sleepiness, and muscle weakness from a lack of oxygen at high altitudes

atmosphere: the layers of gases and other particles that surround Earth and separate the planet from outer space

crevices: cracks or openings in rock

decompose: to disintegrate or break down into smaller parts

geologists: scientists who study rocks, soils, and minerals

hallucinations: false visions or perceptions; things a person sees or feels that do not exist

monsoon: the seasonal wind of the Indian Ocean, blowing from the southwest in the summer, and from the northeast in the winter

surveyors: people who explore and map regions

tectonic plates: large pieces of Earth's crust that move and may collide

tree line: the zone, at high altitudes, beyond which no trees grow

troposphere: the lowest layer of the atmosphere where clouds and weather occur

Index

Log on to www.av2books.com

AV^2 by Weigl brings you media enhanced books that support active learning. Go to www.av2books.com, and enter the special code found on page 2 of this book. You will gain access to enriched and enhanced content that supplements and complements this book. Content includes video, audio, weblinks, quizzes, a slideshow, and activities.

AV^2 Online Navigation

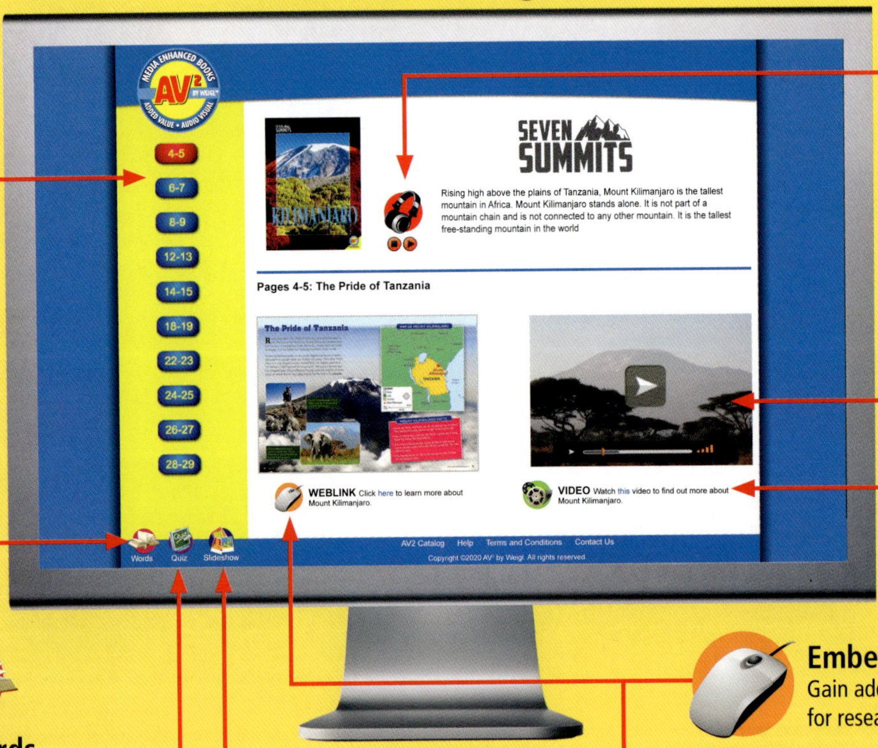

Audio
Listen to sections of the book read aloud

Book Pages
AV^2 pages directly correspond to pages in the book.

Video
Watch informative video clips.

Embedded Weblinks
Gain additional information for research.

Key Words
Study vocabulary, and complete a matching word activity.

Try This!
Complete activities and hands-on experiments.

Quizzes
Test your knowledge.

Slideshow
View images and captions, and prepare a presentation.

AV^2 was built to bridge the gap between print and digital. We encourage you to tell us what you like and what you want to see in the future.

Sign up to be an AV^2 Ambassador at www.av2books.com/ambassador.

Due to the dynamic nature of the internet, some of the URLs and activities provided as part of AV^2 by Weigl may have changed or ceased to exist. AV^2 by Weigl accepts no responsibility for any such changes. All media enhanced books are regularly monitored to update addresses and sites in a timely manner. Contact AV^2 by Weigl at 1-866-649-3445 or av2books@weigl.com with any questions, comments, or feedback.